Symbols of America

THE WHITE HOUSE

Kim Thompson

Norwood House Press

Cataloging-in-Publication Data

Names: Thompson, Kim.
Title: The White House / Kim Thompson.
Description: Buffalo, NY : Norwood House Press, 2026. | Series: Symbols of America | Includes glossary and index.
Identifiers: ISBN 9781978575882 (pbk.) | ISBN 9781978575899 (library bound) | ISBN 9781978575905 (ebook)
Subjects: LCSH: White House (Washington, D.C.)--Juvenile literature. | Washington (D.C.)--Buildings, structures, etc.--Juvenile literature.
Classification: LCC F204.W5 T466 2026 | DDC 975.3--dc23

Published in 2026 by
Norwood House Press
2544 Clinton Street
Buffalo, NY 14224

Designer: Rhea Magaro

Photo credits: Cover, p. 1 Nate Hovee/Shutterstock.com; p. 3 Katarzyna Hurova/Shutterstock.com; pp. 4, 5 Nadia Yong/Shutterstock.com; pp. 6, 13 Everett Collection/Shutterstock.com; pp. 7, 10, 11, 13 Wikipedia; pp. 8, 9, 12, 14 Library of Congress; p. 15 JDALE12/Shutterstock.com; p. 16 The White House; p. 17 NPS/ Kelsey Graczyk p. 18 Harmony Video Production/Shutterstock.com; p. 19 Sean Pavone/Shutterstock.com; p. 21 Chones

Printed in the United States of America

CPSIA compliance information: Batch #CSNHP26: For further information contact Norwood House Press at 1-800-237-9932.

TABLE OF CONTENTS

THE WHITE HOUSE

The White House stands at 1600 Pennsylvania Avenue in Washington, D.C. The President of the United States lives and works there. The president's family lives there too.

The White House is not a **palace**. It is owned by the American people, not by the president. It is often called the People's House. Some parts are open to the **public**.

HOW IT BEGAN

In 1776, the U.S. declared **independence** from Great Britain and King George III. Americans did not want their new country to have a king. They wanted a **democracy** where the people choose their leaders. A new president would be elected every four or eight years. The president would need a place to live.

The White House was not built yet when George Washington was elected the country's first president. By 1800, it was ready. John Adams was the first president to live there.

In 1814, British soldiers burned part of the White House. Repairs were finished in 1817.

In 1902, the West Wing was added. In 1942, the East Wing was built. These areas have offices for the president and the president's **staff**.

Today, the White House has 132 rooms and 35 bathrooms. It has a movie theater, swimming pool, tennis court, and jogging track. It also has a doctor's office and barbershop.

A SYMBOL OF AMERICA

The Oval Office is in the West Wing. The president works in this famous room with curved walls.

The president sits at the **Resolute** Desk. It was given to President Rutherford B. Hayes by British Queen Victoria in 1880. It is made of wood from an old British ship, HMS *Resolute*.

The East Room is the biggest room in the White House. This grand space is used to **host** balls, dinners, and concerts when leaders from around the world come to meet with the president.

Green spaces surround the White House. The president sometimes gives speeches in the Rose Garden. This is also where the president **pardons** a turkey each year for Thanksgiving.

In the spring, children are invited to come to the White House lawn for the Easter Egg Roll.

The White House is a **symbol** of America. Both things were created in the late 1700s. Both were built for the country's people. Both represent a democratic government.

Can you think of other ways that the White House is like the United States?

SPOT THE SYMBOL

If you look closely, you will see the White House on many things related to America. It is on U.S. **currency**, including on the back of the 20 dollar bill. It is on stamps. It is featured in many movies and TV shows.

THE UNITED STATES OF AMERICA
IN GOD WE TRUST
THE WHITE HOUSE
TWENTY DOLLARS
20

GLOSSARY

currency (KUR-uhn-see): money, including coins and paper bills

democracy (di-MAH-kruh-see): a government in which the people choose their leaders

host (hohst): to entertain guests at your home

independence (in-di-PEN-duhns): freedom; self-rule

palace (PAL-is): a large, grand residence owned by a king, queen, or other ruler

pardons (PAHR-dunhz): forgives or cancels a punishment; the turkey pardoned by the president is not eaten at Thanksgiving

public (PUHB-lik): ordinary people

resolute (REZ-uh-loot): strongly determined to do something

staff (staf): people who work for an organization

symbol (SIM-buhl): an object or design that stands for, suggests, or represents something else

THINKING QUESTIONS

1. Who owns the White House?
2. Who was the first president to live in the White House?
3. Name two rooms in the White House.
4. What happens in the Rose Garden?
5. Where can you find the White House on money?

INDEX

ABOUT THE AUTHOR

Kim Thompson is a teacher and writer from Columbus, Ohio. She is an American history buff. She loves to travel to look at statues, monuments, and museums. She thinks it would be fun to do a scavenger hunt to search for symbols of the United States.